Color Your Future

The First Ever Vision Board Coloring Book

Color Your Future. The First Ever Vision Board Coloring Book is perfectly suited for vision board classes and workshops. It is also an excellent, self-contained vision board book that can be used by an individual for enjoyment and personal growth.

Published by Chalcedony Press, Ellicott City, Maryland. U.S.A.

Judith T. Krauthamer

ISBN: 9780989503532

For more information and correspondence, visit www.quietspacecoaching.com

Table of Contents

Introduction

A vision board is a picture, composed of many images, that represents a desired future. Creating a vision board is a first step towards looking at one's life with a sense of control and wonder. It contributes to living a more purposeful life. A <u>coloring</u> vision board helps us to identify our future self by engaging in the meditative and creative act of bringing pens, crayons, and pencils to paper.

We all want a life that is filled with feelings of joy and thoughts that bring us a deep, satisfying sense of well being. If we were to create a picture of those feelings and thoughts, it would be a collage. The collage might include images of physical and mental health, adventure, travel, love, home, and spiritual growth. It may include pictures of a shift in work or a vast change in life's direction. It is a collage that represents hope, beliefs, longings, and desire for a better, more fulfilling life. The collage is aptly called a "Vision Board."

<u>How do I create a vision board?</u>

A vision board is made by compiling images of what you would like to be or have in the future. The images are then assembled in a design that forms a collage. **Color Your Future** provides a wide range of images—pictures, words and sayings— from which you can readily choose many representations of your desired future self. In your coloring book, select an image, saying or word. Color it, cut it out, and attach it to either a back page in the coloring book, or to another piece of paper or poster board.

<u>Why a COLORING vision board?</u>

The act of coloring is meditative. It is a relaxing art form that allows your brain to be creative and contemplative at the same time. When we color we embody, or physically take in, the feelings and thoughts that the picture represents. Coloring generates wellness, quietness and concentration. By combining coloring with compiling pictures and words that represent our future lives, we are connecting and committing to a deeper, more directed, meaningful life.

When you create a personalized vision board and place it in a space where you see it often, you are consciously reminded of the envisioned person you want to grow into. The colored vision board becomes a powerful tool that serves as your image of the future - a tangible representation of where you are going. It represents your dreams, your goals, and your ideal life. The beauty of a *Color Your Future* vision board is that you can witness, each and every day, the steps and actions you are taking towards achieving this ideal future.

The perfect Tool for Conducting a Vision Board Workshop

Using the *Color Your Future* coloring book is an upbeat, fun and personal way to have a successful vision board workshop. There are two different ways to use this coloring book for a workshop.

1. Give each participant their own *Color Your Future* coloring book. You would include the price of the book in the cost of the workshop. Have pencils, pens, scissors and glue/tape available for the participants.
2) Make copies of the pages of the coloring book. The advantage of this coloring book is that I release the copyright—in other words, you are encouraged to copy and distribute the graphics in this book! You can choose how many copies you would like to make and how you would like to distribute or display the graphics in the workshop room. This allows you to take control of your inventory, based on how many people are attending the workshop.

Easy Steps for Conducting a Color Your Future Vision Board Workshop

The coloring book is divided into sections. These sections represent the top ten areas that people point to when making vision boards. They are viewed as the most important components of their life. They are: career, education, personal growth, finances, glamour, health, travel, home, spirituality, and relationships. I have added an eleventh section, words to live by. These words stand out as personality descriptors that people identify with.

Each section has its own introduction page. Each section's introductory page has a short exercise that gives the participant an opportunity to spend a few minutes exploring what is personally meaningful. One option for the workshop is to have participants fill out all of the introductory pages at the start of the workshop. Encouraging your group to think about their goals and values through this exercise sets the stage for creating a vision board that is closely aligned with each attendee's deepest sense of self.

Each individual can use the workbook in the way that best suits them. Whether they are using their own coloring book or copied pages set out on a table, the attendees choose the graphics that resonate with them. There is an additional page, My Words, My Art, for attendees to add their own inspiration. They then color, cut and attach the images onto the last page of *Color Your Future* or on paper or poster board.

Color Your Future for yourself

Although designed for workshop use, this coloring book is well suited to an individual creating a personalized, colored vision board. Simply follow the same steps as if you were taking a coloring vision board workshop. Fill out the questionnaires that are at the beginning of each section to help clarify values and inner wisdom. Then go through the book and select the graphics that speak to you. You can choose to paste your images in the back of *Color Your Future* or onto another piece of paper.

Using the Coloring Vision Board

The graphics are small enough that you can paste them in the back of the book or onto a single sheet of paper. It can be folded and carried in your purse or wallet. Let it be your daily reminder of the person you want to be, and the environment you want to live in. It is your personal, visual reminder of the person you are—the inner person, who desires joy, happiness and fulfillment. It reminds you that you can achieve these things by remaining focused on the goals. "This is what I want. This is how I get there."

Enjoy! *Judy*

In partnership,
Judith T. Krauthamer
www.quietspacecoaching.com

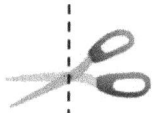

Three Dream Jobs

1. _____

_____

_____

2. _____

_____

_____

3. _____

_____

_____

More
Networking

My next job will be my dream job

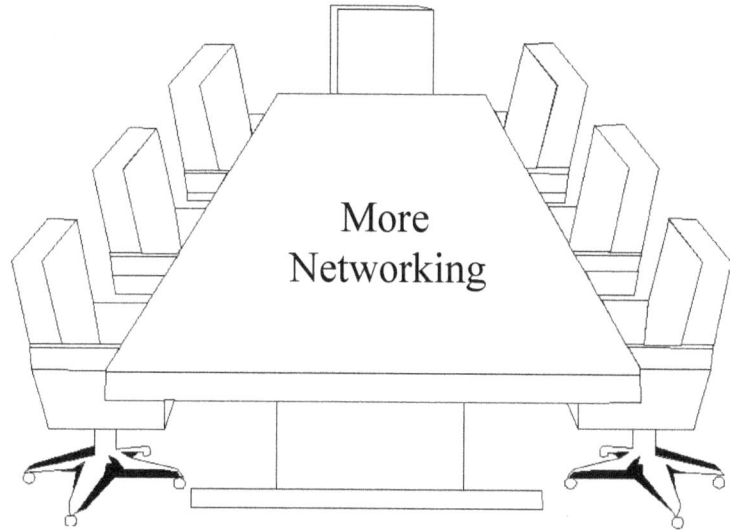

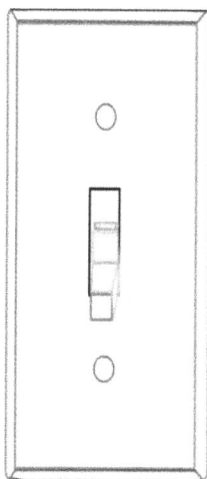

Switch
Careers

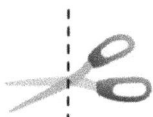

BOSS

My ideas matter

Start A Business

Write My Book

A New Direction

Be MY OWn BOSS

New

Partnerships

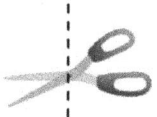

My Five-Year Goals

1. _____

_____

_____

2. _____

_____

_____

3. _____

_____

_____

_____

Going back to school

I'm a lifelong learner

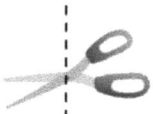

New Way of Thinking

Take new classes

get my degree

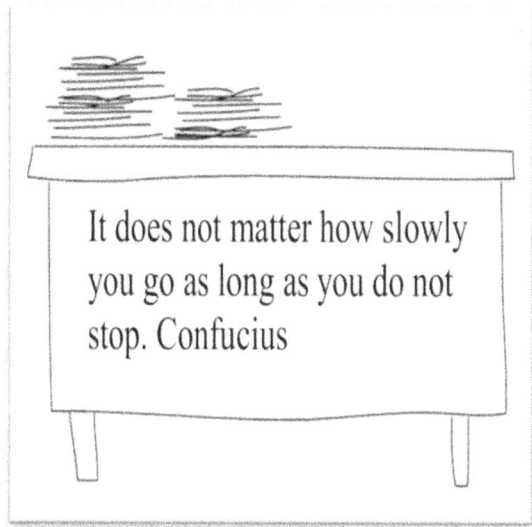

It does not matter how slowly you go as long as you do not stop. Confucius

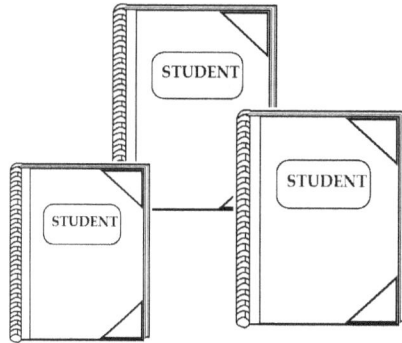

STUDENT

STUDENT

STUDENT

Explore webinars
and
online workshops

Personal Growth Personal Growth

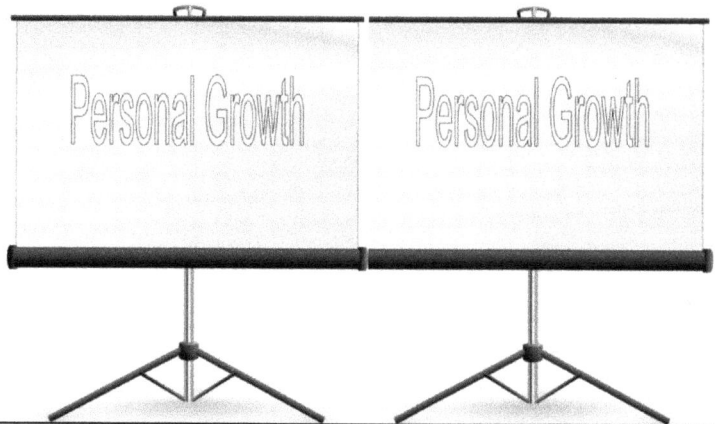

My inner wisdom says:

1. _____

_____

_____

2. _____

_____

_____

3. _____

_____

_____

I Weigh My Options

I am powerful

Be Brave

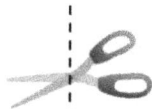

**Move
Through
Grief**

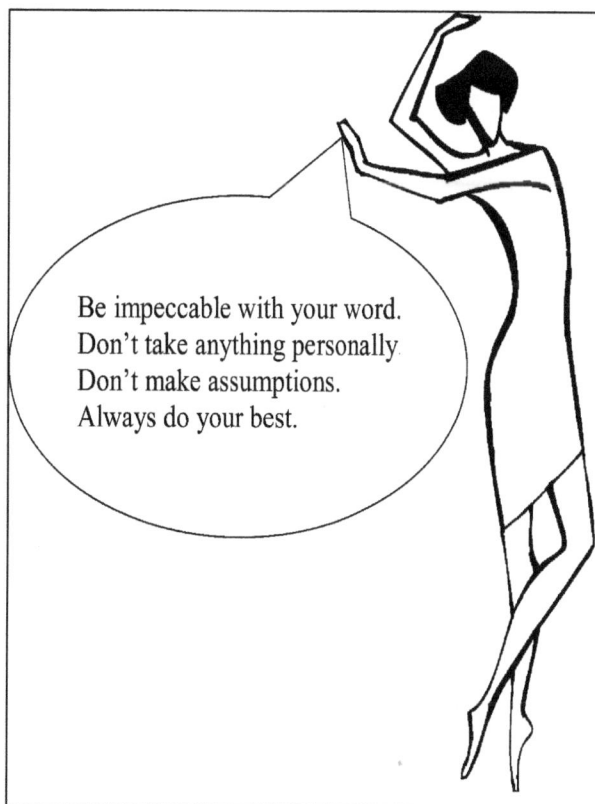

May I love
and accept myself
just as I am.

Be impeccable with your word.
Don't take anything personally.
Don't make assumptions.
Always do your best.

I have the power
to change my mind
and change
my life.

Rest
and Relax

Do one thing every
day that scares you.
Eleanor Roosevelt

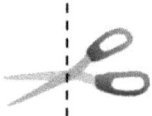

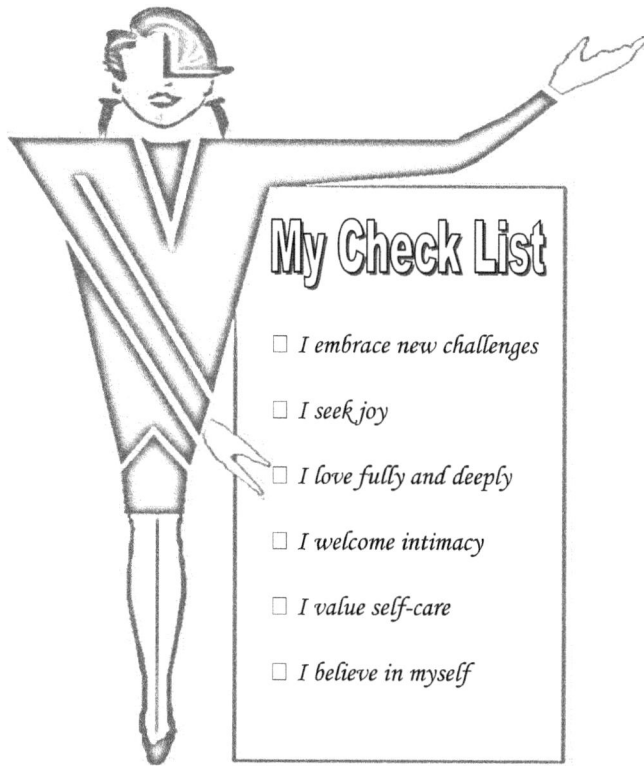

My Check List

☐ I embrace new challenges

☐ I seek joy

☐ I love fully and deeply

☐ I welcome intimacy

☐ I value self-care

☐ I believe in myself

I
LET
GO
OF
FEAR

Finances Finances

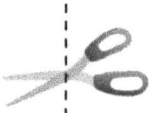

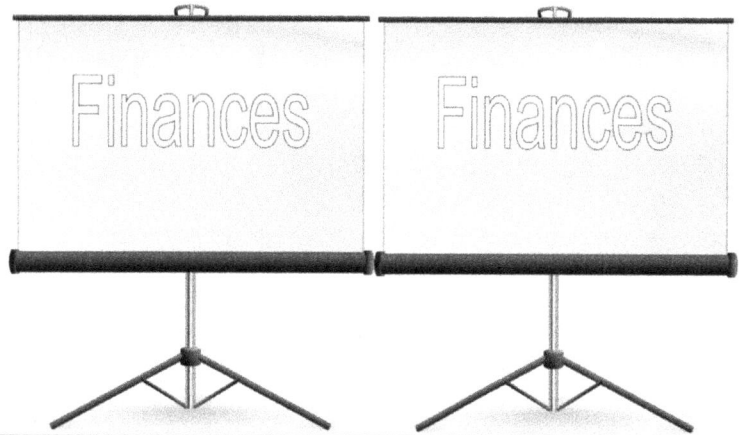

Financial Security Means:

1. _____

_____

_____

2. _____

_____

_____

3. _____

_____

_____

I build a nest egg

Investments

Save for a Rainy Day

Debt-FREE

I set boundaries and protect what is mine.

Glamour Glamour

What makes me feel glamorous:

1. _____

_____

2. _____

_____

3. _____

_____

My true beauty
lies within

The
Real
Me

I am changing
my self-image

Watch out world. Here I come.

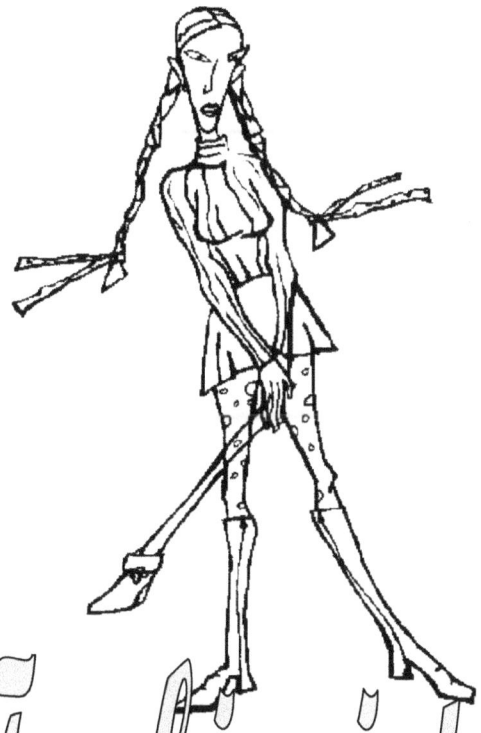

beautiful

Fashionista

I don't let other people define my style

Dress for Success

I dress to express my true self.

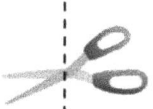

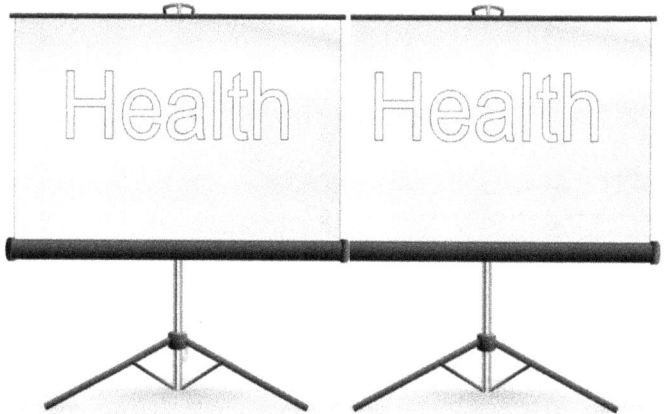

Good Health means:

1. _____

   _____

   _____

2. _____

   _____

   _____

3. _____

   _____

   _____

Better Choices

SALAD

Pain-Free

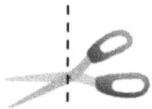

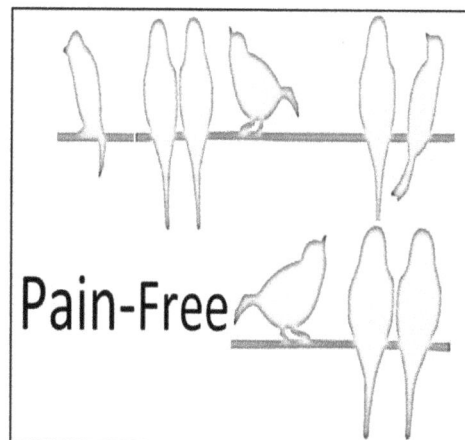

The most certain way to succeed is always to try just one more time.
Thomas A. Edison

Self-Care

I let go of the urge to criticize my body

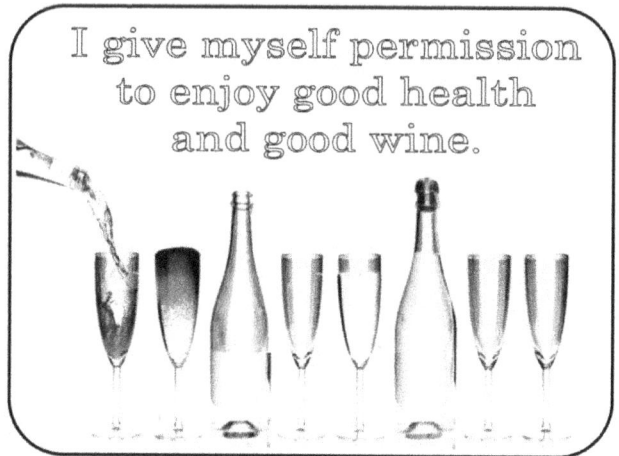

I give myself permission to enjoy good health and good wine.

My favorite things about home are:

1. _____

   _____

   _____

2. _____

   _____

   _____

3. _____

   _____

   _____

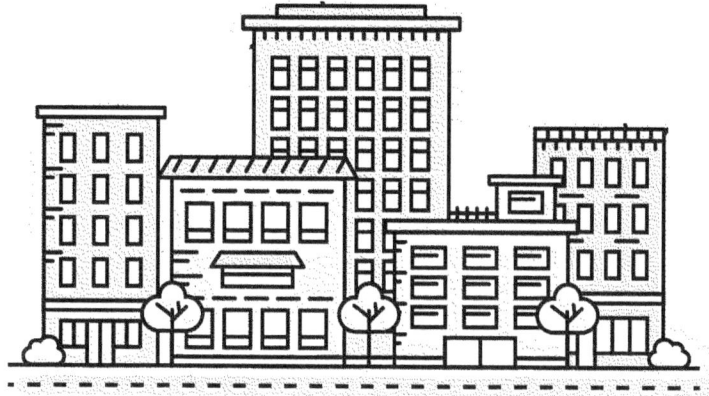

My Own Apartment

Getting Organized!

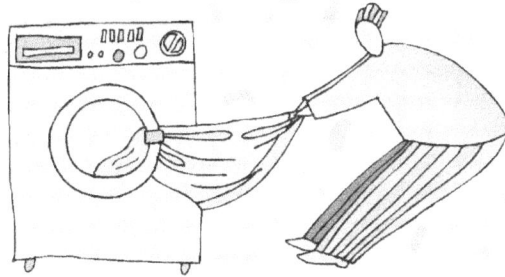

A Fabulous New Kitchen

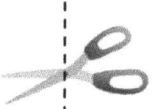

REDECORATE

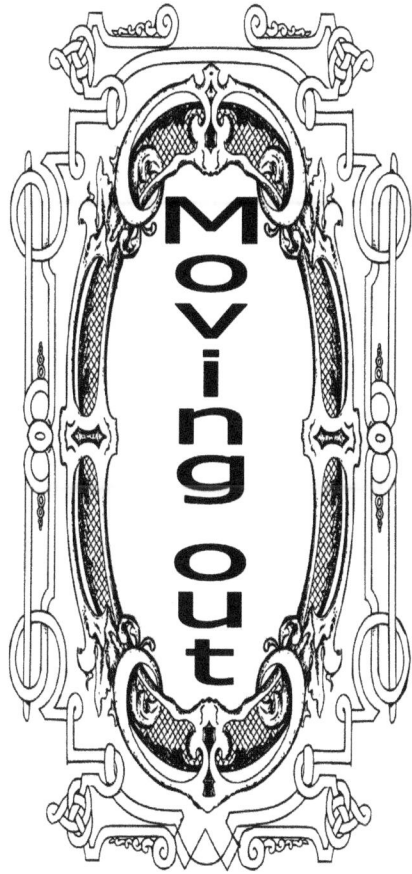

Moving out

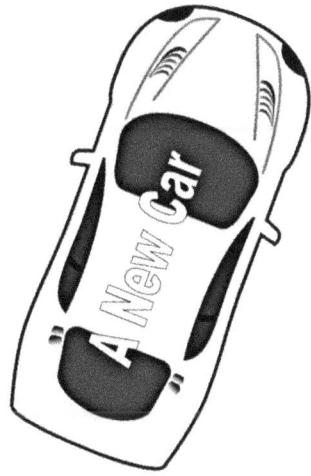

A New Car

61

A Home
Of My
Own

No More
Mortgage
Payments

Spirituality Spirituality

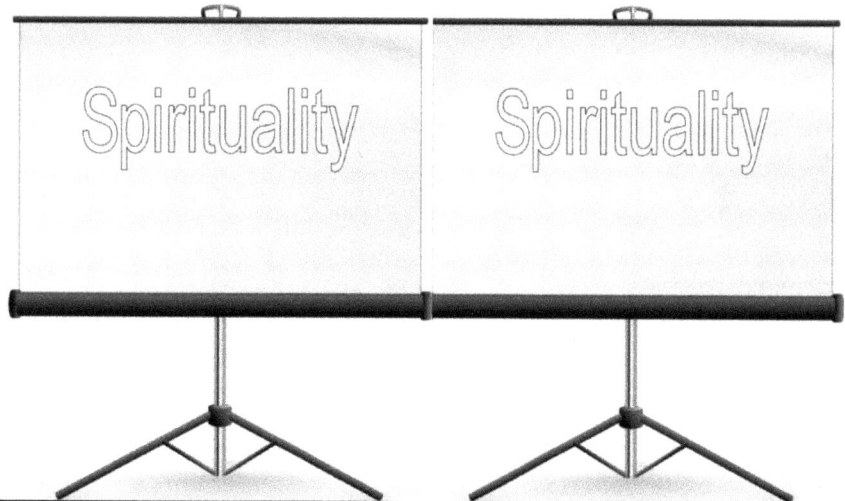

My core spiritual beliefs:

1. _____

_____

_____

_____

2. _____

_____

_____

3. _____

_____

_____

_____

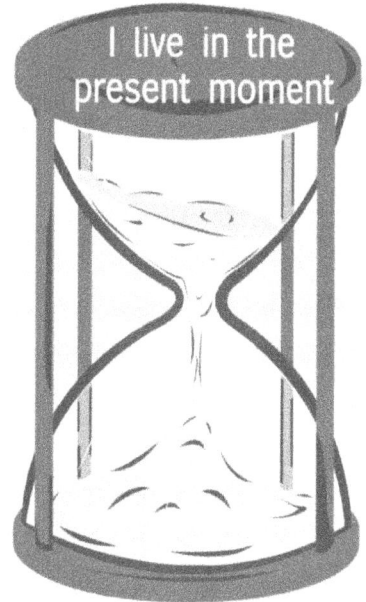

I live in the present moment

Letting Go

COURAGEOUS

FREE

You
Become
What
You
Believe

Peace of Mind

What we think, we become. Buddha

A Deeper Faith

My top five places to visit:

1. _____

2. _____

3. _____

4. _____

5. _____

I treat myself to a vacation

Around the World

Adventure

Visit The Exotic

Going Places

Camping Out

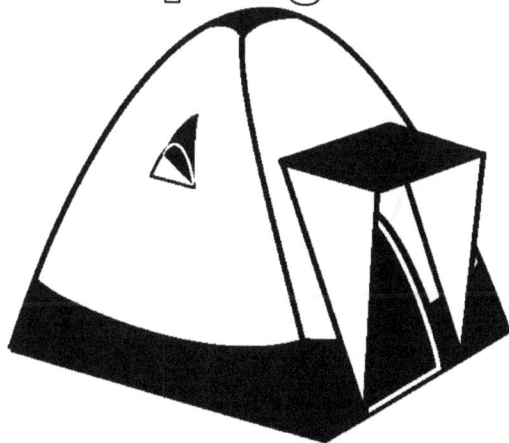

Next stop:
A different city

I fulfill
my
bucket list

life is a beach

Relationships Relationships

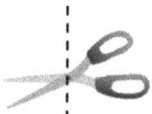

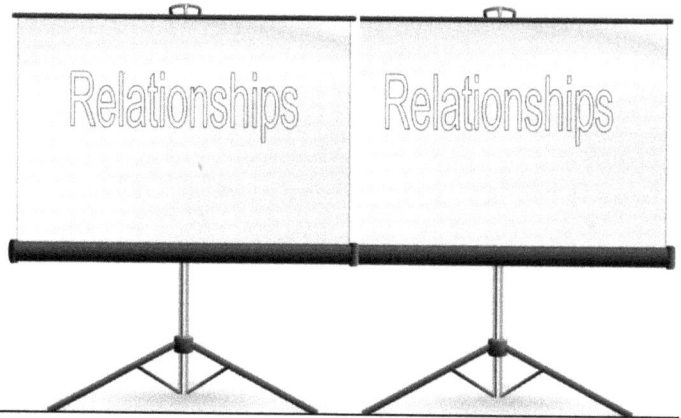

My most important relationships are:

1. _____

2. _____

3. _____

4. _____

5. _____

Marriage

Family

Renew Friendships

I
Stay
Connected

I learn
how to say
I'm sorry.

I will follow where love leads me

Words To
Live By

Words To
Live By

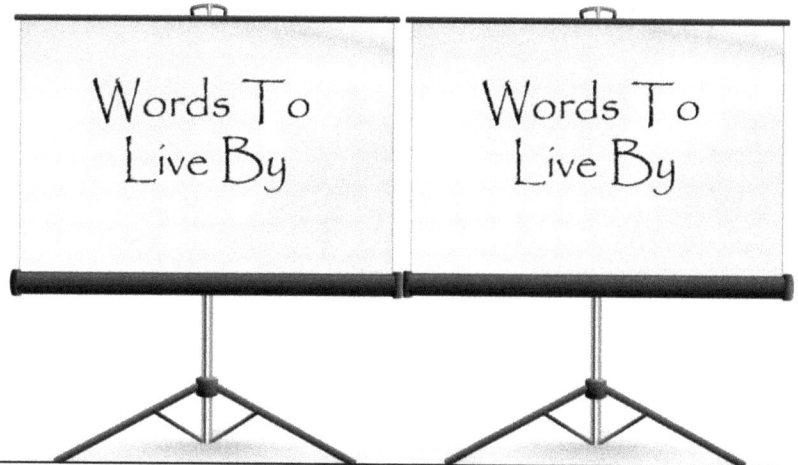

Check all that apply:

☐ I will take steps to create changes

☐ I will say "I love you" more often

☐ I will apologize when I am wrong

☐ I will show myself more kindness

☐ I will look at my fears so that I can overcome them

☐ I will acknowledge my bravery

☐ I will tell myself "I am worthy" more often

☐ I will learn how to manage my anger

☐ I look forward to a fabulous future

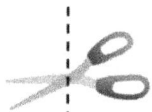

Gratitude

Serenity

Hopeful

Bravery

Kindness

Eager

Compassion

Curious

Wide-Awake

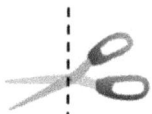

Sexy

Radiant

Dazzled

Calm

Joyous

Mellow

Buoyant Focused

My Vision

Board

Date_____

My Words, My Art

9780989503532